EARLY
ONTARIO
GRAVESTONES

EARLY ONTARIO GRAVESTONES

Carole Hanks

McGRAW-HILL RYERSON LIMITED

Toronto   Montreal   New York   London   Sydney
Johannesburg   Mexico   Panama   Düsseldorf
Singapore   São Paulo   Kuala Lumpur   New Delhi

EARLY ONTARIO GRAVESTONES

ISBN 0-07-077765-9

LCCCN 73-21056

1 2 3 4 5 6 7 8 9 10 AP 3 2 1 0 9 8 7 6 5 4

Printed and bound in Canada

Contents

Settlers and Gravestones

In the last decades of the eighteenth century Canada was still a raw, open land, free of the influence of European culture, inhabited by a people whose way of life did not require the taming of nature.

It was to this open land, populated only sparsely by their fellow countrymen, that the early settlers came. They came by sea from Europe and by land from the United States. They settled where there was arable land and potable water. Often they grouped together, forming small communities within close distance of already established trading posts or miliary forts. With a haste born of necessity the towns grew; and the ever greater numbers of people who came to the new land were inclined to take up residence on parcels of land some distance from the nearest settlement.

"The bush," the English called it, this almost untouched land. To get to it they rode in carts pulled by oxen, and crossed bodies of water in small river craft, shifting their worldly possessions from one vehicle to the next until they reached their destination. Although a homestead may have been only three or four miles from the nearest town, the path to be travelled was often so tortuous that the journey was not lightly undertaken. Roads were merely openings through bush and forest, narrowing to nothing in particularly dense areas and blocked by the occasional tree felled either carelessly by man or inadvertently by nature. Once in the bush, trips out were made mainly from need, and visits from neighbors were important occasions. Often these neighborly visits revolved around the offering or gaining of assistance. With such help, log houses were built, land cleared and crops grown, harvested and stored, often within a season. As raw as the new land was, it was made comfortably habitable with astonishing dispatch. In effect, it was rather abruptly civilized.

This rapid growth and development can be seen in the artifacts that come down to us from that time. They show no evidence of leisurely evolution through centuries of aesthetic evaluation and exploration. Eighteenth and nineteenth century Europe was a modern civilization, and goods from long-established nations were imported to Canada in quantity; so that when these new Canadians manufactured their own goods, the goods took the form of the familiar objects brought from the old land. The differences were chiefly due to lack of technology, and often from lack of craftsmen skilled in particular trades.

Much of the eighteenth and nineteenth century Canadiana has long since disappeared. Household items, including furniture, are perishable, being relatively small and used daily. Architecture is more durable, but the human penchant for progress has ensured its disappearance also. Of all the early Canadian artifacts, tombstones are the ones most certainly created to endure. Commemoration of the dead, respect for memory and love of individuals are powerful forces in human nature. These feelings, often embodied in religious piety, have always made funerary art a carefully considered and beautifully crafted form, regardless of culture. Canada was no exception. Now our technological expertise has brought the funerary art form to an impasse of mass-produced and dull uniformity; but one hundred years ago gravestones were objects of pleasing form and decoration, meant to be enjoyed by the living and, as well, pay respect to the dead.

The last decade of the eighteenth century saw the beginning of a particular type of gravestone that, until the end of the nineteenth century, represents a distinct style readily distinguishable from twentieth century grave markers in form and decoration.

This old form is basically a rectangular slab, with variations in shape occurring only at the upper quarter of the stone. Very few early examples of the non-slab type exist. While obelisks, columns, and an occasional angel or geometric form were erected as early as the middle of the nineteenth century, they are uncommon enough to be seen as representing merely a desire for individuality.

Both slab and sculptural forms are traditional, reaching back as far as preclassical Greece. They were brought to Canada from older cultures in England and continental Europe and also transmitted through the then young culture of the United States, which had, in turn, adopted the forms from the Old World. Though both forms are traditional, it is obvious that the slab type was greatly preferred or it would not exist in such vast numbers in the older cemeteries today. Such an overwhelming preference for this particular type was likely for practical economic reasons as well as aesthetic ones. The sculptural markers, being three-dimensional forms, are larger and heavier than the slab markers and therefore more difficult to quarry and transport, as well as more costly. Most ordinary citizens would not have been able to afford costly grave markers.

Although the markers vary from one to six feet in height, they are most often three and a half to four feet tall and two feet wide. Surface decoration is rarely as austere as that seen on modern gravestones. Epitaphs, descriptive inscriptions and decorative motifs were often employed on a single marker. Existing markers are almost exclusively of stone, as only in rare instances have wooden markers dating back to the nineteenth century survived to the present.

The earliest markers found in Ontario date from the 1790s. It would appear surprising at first that earlier examples do not occur, for settlers were moving into Ontario from the Detroit area and from the east certainly as early as 1750. But pioneer life was not conducive to elaborate burial practices. A few words spoken over a simple grave dug by a member of the deceased's family probably had to suffice in an existence that was daily concerned with the making of food and the maintenance of shelter. It is likely that the earliest graves were marked with a simple wooden plaque or not at all. Wood was readily available, easily cut and easily carved, but in its raw state and in small pieces it rots rapidly when exposed to weather. Isolation was also a factor in the present scarcity of grave markers from the earliest period of settlement. Isolation made necessary the burial of the dead on the nearest convenient plot of land. Subsequently, the land may have been kept as a family burying ground, or been abandoned for a community burying ground in later years. In either case, the graves themselves have been lost to the interested passer-by. Thus, allowance must be made not only for the perishability of wood and the harshness of life that may have precluded the use of grave markers altogether, but also for the possibility of neglect of small family burying grounds. Left untended, markers are rapidly covered by vegetation and are lost to view.

About 1900 the block-like markers of the present day gained favor, replacing the rectangular slab variety that had been popular for the previous one hundred years.

These modern markers soon lost their individual character in the interests of brevity, mounting costs and a new aesthetic that had a horror of sentimentalizing. They soon became little more than stone name plates.

Materials

With the exception of the few wooden markers extant, all
nineteenth century Ontario grave markers are made of
stone, the most common type being a soft variety of white
marble that weathers fairly rapidly and unevenly. Its
granular structure is loosened by water, causing it to fall
away bit by bit. The result is a rough, sugary-looking
surface. As the stone seems to weather away most rapidly
along the edges of the carving, small lettering is often
illegible, if not completely erased, after a hundred years.

Sandstone and slate, finer and more closely grained
stones than the soft marble, were also used, though not
so much as the marble. Although both stand up well
against the weather, sandstone is susceptable to exfoliation,
a weathering process in which the stone is sheared off
layer by layer until nothing but the thinnest slab remains.

Granite, a stone used almost exclusively for modern
monuments because of its hardness and durability, was
used only on rare occasions for nineteenth century markers.
Because of its hardness it was difficult to carve by hand
and difficult to quarry, and thus too costly.

The soft quality of most of these stones, along with the
technique of high relief carving employed in the motifs,
precludes the possibility of getting reasonably good
rubbings from nineteenth century markers.

Gravestone rubbings are made by passing a pencil,
crayon or other marker over the surafce of a paper that
has been placed on the surface of the stone. Areas that
are carved into the stone, lying thus below the surface, do
not receive the weight of the crayon and remain as white

areas on the paper. All other sections pick up the color of the marker. When the outer edges of the carving are not sharp, if the relief of the carving is too high, or if the surface of the stone is too rough, the resulting print is a bold texture of dots and smudges. This may be an accurate document of the uneven surface of the stone, but it is an illegible record of man's efforts to carve that stone.

More sophisticated methods of picking up the image could be used, but they require methods of inking that would deface the gravestone, a process that is discouraged when one is dealing with the property of others.

The slate markers of New England and the few slate markers in Ontario that are carved in the same etching technique are well suited to rubbing. With some practice, one may obtain a satisfactory print from such stones.

With little exception all the above-mentioned stones were imported to Ontario. Quarries in western New England yielded marble and slate. Marble, the overwhelming favorite, was sometimes imported from even more distant sources. In 1864 the R. Sheppard Marble and Stone Works firm of Toronto advertised monuments of Italian marble as well as the more usual American variety.

The extent to which much of this marble has weathered in the past one hundred to one hundred and eighty years is unfortunate. Rain and snow are certainly the primary factors in this deterioration process. Fungus growth and neglect are important secondary aspects. Fungus obliterates surface carving and eventually eats away the stone itself. Neglect of care and attention to cemetery grounds enables vegetation to overrun the markers, hiding the cemetery from view and eventually destroying the stone by the natural action of root growth and water seepage.

There are areas of the province in which marble slabs of similar age are decidedly less weathered than in others. The modern problem of industrial chemical pollution has some bearing on this phenomenon. Airborne chemical fumes such as sulphur dioxide can hasten the deterioration of stone and wood. Because of the present accelerated pace of such pollution, one need not look only to the earliest industrial areas for severely eroded gravestones. Any area of heavy industry and high population density, such as Hamilton or Toronto, can pump enough effluent into the air to cause late nineteenth century markers to resemble early nineteenth century stones elsewhere. A variety of factors come into play in the problem of industrial pollution, of course. Prevailing winds and general weather conditions, the contour of the land, the type of effluent being put into the air, and density of industrial waste in proportion to the surrounding area are all factors in the rate of deterioration. In this context it is interesting to note that both wooden and stone grave markers in Moosonee are in an excellent state of preservation.

Techniques and Craftsmen

The very earliest stone markers in Ontario are crudely
worked. They are roughly slabbed and shaped fieldstones
onto which are carved initials and a date. The carving on
these stones is always uneven in spacing, depth of cut
and slant of letters. Within ten years these rudely crafted
markers were replaced by ones showing far greater even-
ness of lettering and cutting and a greater length of
inscription, including the full name of the deceased person,
dates of birth and death and often some kind of epitaph.
Although the workmanship in this second stage of gravestone development is far more proficient than in the
earlier, there is still a slight unevenness to the lettering,
and there are no decorative motifs to enhance the inscription. It is the rudimentary craftsmanship of these few
early markers that affords our only glmpse at a possible
development of style and technique on Ontario gravestones.
For when slab markers appear in abundance around the
1820s and 1830s they are a product of professional
competence, i.e. the lettering is evenly spaced and the depth
of the cut is uniform throughout the wealth of inscription.
Full names, dates of birth and death, family relationships
and poetic epitaphs are found. Rarely are these markers
without an additional decorative motif, expertly carved
in a representational style.

Because of the great difference in workmanship among
grave markers separated in time by no more than thirty
years, it would appear that the technical competence
apparent in the later ones was less a result of a develop-
mental pattern than of individual competence. For when

stylistic and technical development are considered it is in terms of lifetimes and generations; there must be time for styles to be thought through, varied, and reworked into new forms which are eventually accepted by others. Thirty years is too brief a time span for this kind of deliberation and evolution of style; it is too brief a time span for the widespread distribution of an upgraded technical skill. The situation of the earliest settlers must be understood in this context. If a gravestone was to be carved for an individual in a relatively isolated place, the carving would, of necessity, be done by someone in the near vicinity. This means that some of the earliest markers were carved by a member of the family or a friend likely not trained as a stone carver. It is no wonder that the result was crude. With the appearance of skillful, professional workmanship in the 1820s and 1830s it can be assumed that the professional monument carver had arrived on the Ontario frontier.

From mid-nineteenth century on there are numerous examples of gravestones on which the craftsman's name and address have been carved, a sure sign of professionalism, though not the only one. It is now difficult to determine whether or not this was standard practice, as many gravestones have settled deeply into the ground, concealing any information at their base. Standard practice or not, there are sufficient examples to ascertain that most Ontario markers were locally carved, i.e. the monument carver lived in the town for which he made monuments, or at least in a nearby town. Exceptions are found only occasionally in which a stone was carved in the United States.

Wooden mallets and steel chisels were the usual tools used to carve early markers. Designs and inscriptions were drawn either directly on the surface of the stone or on a coating made of acacia-gum glue and plaster. The glue and plaster substance created a white surface on which to work and was readily scrubbed off once the stone had been carved.

Carvers of gravestones were known as marble manufacturers or marble cutters. They ran marble factories or marble works. By the present time most of their names have disappeared into history along with any records or collections of sepulchral designs they may have kept. A few may be found listed in old national or provincial directories, but their places of business have long since disappeared. R. Sheppard Marble and Stone Works was located at 171 Queen Street in Toronto. This number now lies approximately at the junction of Queen Street and University Avenue, an area of eight-lane divided macadam and massive granite buildings. The number 171 no longer exists.

Shapes

The shapes the early markers take are widely varied within the rectangular slab format. There were an almost unlimited number of linear outlines that could be applied to the top portion of the stone, a representative sampling of which can be seen in the section of photographs that follows this text. These shapes do not represent a development of style through time, but rather an individual choice of a decorative adjunct to the rest of the marker. The outline shape has no direct design relationship to the decorative motif on the face of the marker, and no symbolic relationship to the epitaph, the religious sect or the deceased. Occasionally a particular shape found favor within a town, and a predominance of that shape is then observable within that town's cemetery. In the Kinsey Bean Cemetery in Doon, for example, the earliest markers have an unusual configuration of curved shapes across the top of the slab. Within a few years that design was no longer popular, and the less ornate marker shapes were used.

Epitaphs

Epitaphs are common on old markers, the most popular form being a four-line verse with alternate lines rhyming. For the most part these verses are standardized, and are repeated again and again on markers across the province. One might guess, in view of such constant repetition, that there was at one time a source for these epitaphs. One possibility would be the existence of books of epitaph verses much like the present-day books of symbolic designs kept for reference by modern monument makers. However, no old source books have yet come to light. A second possibility, and a likely one, is that the epitaph verses were passed by word of mouth from parish to parish and district to district, thus creating an oral tradition.

Given the existing evidence, it is probable that oral tradition played a role in the spread of nineteenth century Ontario epitaphs. They became popular around the middle of the nineteenth century and remained so until the slab type of gravestone fell into disuse. Although instances of epitaphs are not rare before the 1840s, they are by no means as common as they are later on.

Single-line epitaphs and quotes from the Bible were also used. The most common single-line epitaph is part of a Biblical verse: "Blessed are the dead which die in the Lord. . . ." (Revelation 14:13.) Others commonly found are: "May he rest in peace," "Gone but not forgotten," "Not dead but gone before" and "Firm hope of a joyful Resurrection." These single-line epitaphs can display interesting variation and individuality. "Youth and age are snatched away by death's restless hands" is one such variation found on a marker in the Dunville cemetery. "Nip't in the bud to blossom in heaven" is on a child's gravestone in the Hespeler cemetery. "Time how short: Eternity how great:" is carved on a Simcoe marker. While these single-line epitaphs are fairly common, they were never as popular as the four-line verse epitaphs.

One of the single most common verse epitaphs is the following:

A faithful friend a husband dear
A tender parent lieth here;
Great is the loss that we sustain
But hope in heaven to meet again.

With appropriate changes of wording for a mother, this verse is used for women as well, and appears from one end of the province to the other.
A second very common verse is the following:

Kind friends beware as you pass by,
As you now are so once was I,
As I am now so you must be,
Prepare, therefore, to follow me.

The following grim little reminder is also widespread, with minor local variations in wording. It bears no relationship to the age of the deceased, being used for young and old, and it strikes a bitter note:

All you that read with little care
And turn away and leave me here
Remember that you have to die
And be entombed as well as I

(Upper Canada Village,
Pioneer Memorial, 1860)

Despite the universal note struck in many of these epitaphs, they are often altered to suit the individual. Thus the above thought becomes more personal for a young man:

All you dear friends who come my grave to see
Prepare yourselves to follow me.
Prepare yourselves, make no delay
For I in haste was called away.

(Niagara-on-the-Lake, 1867)

With further alteration, the same thought was inscribed on the grave marker of a young woman who died in childbirth:

Farewell my husband and parent dear,
We are not dead but sleeping here.
As we are now so you must be,
Prepare yourselves to follow me.

(Bowmanville, 1852)

There are many young people's graves among the early gravestones—young people's and children's. Childbirth claimed a fair number of women and infants, judging from the numerous markers for both. There were many special children's epitaphs and it seems that a higher percentage of children's graves were marked with epitaphs than were adults'. One of the most common is the following:

Sleep on sweet babe,
And take thy rest,
God cald the home,
For he thought it best.

(Picton, 1855)

The third line should read "God called thee home."
Spelling is not always so casual, although obvious con-
fusion in spelling can be seen from time to time. The
following epitaph is on a marker in the Mohawk Chapel
burying ground: "Though are gone but not forgotten" was
surely meant to read, "Thou are (or art) gone but not
forgotten."

Disease also claimed both young and old. It is no
wonder that another common epitaph refers to this cause
of death:

Friends nor physicians could not save,
This mortal body from the grave;
Nor can the grave confine it here,
When Christ our Saviour shall appear.

(Port Dover, 1861)

Another verse refers to long illness:

Affliction sore long have I bore
Physicians staff was vain
Till God above in tender love
Did relieve me of my pain.

(Bowmanville, 1866)

For all the verses proclaiming sorrow, there are as
many, such as the two above, which end on a hopeful note.
Although none could be considered truly joyful, a few
epitaphs describe a welcome peace:

The pains of death are past
Labor and sorrow ceased
And life's long warfare closed at last
His soul is found in peace.

(Beamsville, 1888)

Individual variations on standardized epitaphs can offer intriguing insights into a personality. The following series illustrates this particularly well:

In death's cold arms lies sleeping here,
A tender parent, a companion dear.
In love she lived, in peace she died.
Her life was asked, but was denied.
>   (Kinsey Bean Pioneer Cemetery,
>   Doon, 1892)

A tender wife a mother dear,
A faithful friend lies buried here;
In love she lived in fear she died,
Her life was asked but God denied.
>   (Upper Canada Village
>   Pioneer Memorial, 1866)

A tender wife a mother dear.
A sincere friend lieth here,
In fear she lived in hope she died,
Her life was asked but God denied.
>   (Williamsburg, 1872)

Of the more individualized epitaphs, such as the ones above, it is difficult to discern whether they too were part of the standard repertoire or if they were composed solely for the person on whose marker they were carved. They frequently followed the standard form, being altered only slightly. The question then is whether or not these verses were composed for the individual, altered to fit the individual, or inadvertently altered by oral tradition. There is not enough remaining evidence to give weight to a

statistical study correlating frequency of alterations
with their dates.

A further example of personalized epitaphs is the
following, found on the marker of a woman who died in
her late 70s:

What though her aged form decay,
And moulder in the tomb.
Her spirit lies in realms of day,
Enjoying endless bloom.
                              (Crosshill, 1871)

Further, this verse was found on the gravestone of a
thirty-one-year-old man:

Tis hard to die so young, just verging
On manhood's happy joyous days—
To die when [hopes we feel are] urging,
When life is bright as summer's rays.
                              (Adolphustown, 1863)

The words in brackets are nearly illegible and thus are an
uncertain transcription.

A verse for a little girl referred not only to the child and
her age but also to the bird carved on the marker:

Beloved, lovely,
She was but seven.
A fair bird to earth,
To blossom in heaven.
                              (Picton, 1877)

The following longer verse was on a single stone for both husband and wife, and records the stern religious belief they held:

O'er 50 yrs. we struggled here,
Together through this world of woe.
Each one the burden freely bore,
Through summer's heat, and winter's snow.
But now the struggle's past and gone,
We hope the debt of sin is paid.
And in the resurrection morn,
To awake in Christ our living head.
(Bowmanville, 1872)

A departure from the standard four-line verse was found on a marker for a woman. It was signed, which is unusual, with the letter "T":

Stay, gentle reader stay—
Pl Drop a pitying tear,
The best of Mothers
Wives, and Friends,
Lies here
(Grimsby, 1814)

The "Pl" is an abbreviation for please.

Names are seldom incorporated into a verse epitaph, but when they are the entire verse seems more personal, less an altered version of a standard sentiment:

William's sweet smiles no more will see,
His voice no more on earth we'll hear,
From earth, with all its cares he's freed,
Though causing many a silent tear.

(Trenton, 1867)

A marker with an unusually long inscription was found
in the cemetery between Union and Sparta. It contains
three separate epitaphs, which appear to be a combination
of a conventional verse and specially composed epitaphs.
The interesting aspect of these verses is found in the final
lines, where the writer professes uncertainty about a
better world after death:

An honest man here lies at rest,
As e'er God with his image blest.
The friend of man, the friend of truth,
The friend of age and guide of youth.

He was a good Neighbour,
An affectionate Husband,
A kind Father,
And a faithful Friend.

Few hearts like his, with virtue warm'd
Few heads with knowledge so inform'd
If there's another world he lives in bliss
If there is none he made the best of this.

(Union/Sparta, 1848)

For all the charm of the verse epitaphs, they are rarely
as informative about the deceased's life or death as are
those written in prose. A particuarly interesting example
of such prose is an epitaph found on a marker in Windsor:

SACRED
to the memory of
John James Hume Esqre M.D.
Staff assistant Surgeon
who was inhumanly murdered and his bo
dy afterwards brutally mangled by a ga
ng of armed ruffians from the United States
styling themselves
PATRIOTS
who committed this cowardly and shameful outrage
on the morning of the 4th December 1838 having
intercepted the deceased while proceeding to render
professional assistance to Her Majesty's gallant
Militia engaged at Windsor U.C. in repelling
the incursions of this rebel crew more properly styled
PIRATES
(Windsor, 1838)

The stone is a large one, so large that it lies flat on the ground. It is in such excellent condition that one may assume that its surface has been cleaned and perhaps recarved recently. The format is original, however, judging from the lack of concern about cutting words in half in order to fit all the information into the given space. Such lack of attention to written form is common on markers carved during the first half of the nineteenth century and earlier; it is unheard of on twentieth century markers. Also, as space runs out, the lettering in the second block of prose, after the word PATRIOTS, is considerably more cramped and slightly smaller than in the first block.

An example of a prose epitaph that gives some insight into the personality of the deceased is the following,

barely legible, inscription on an eighteenth century
marker in Adolphustown:

Here lies Entomb$_d$
Hannah
Van-Dusen
Who deceased
March 8
1791
27 Yr. . . . Mth. . . . D.
She was the wife of . . .
rud Van Dusen: and faith-
fully discharged the duties of
a Companion a Parent
and a Citizen

Once again, the emphasis is on content rather than
written form. Abbreviations were often used to enable
given information to be fitted into the space available.
If even then there was not enough room, smaller letters,
shallowly carved, were inserted over the last line of the
sentence in which they were to be included. An example of
this technique can be seen in the Anglican churchyard at
Niagara-on-the-Lake, which marks the grave of a
four-year-old girl.

My time is short the longer my rest
best
God calld me hence because he thought
So wep not drie up your tears
Heare must I be till Christ appears
(Niagara-on-the-Lake, 1802)

The word "best," as well as the final letters on the words

"thought" and "appears," are squeezed in above the lines in which they would normally appear. As is the case with many of the very early markers this one has a particular charm because of its laboriously uneven lettering and obvious misspellings. It brings to mind the necessarily simple life of Canadian pioneer days in which an inexperienced individual might have found it necessary to make a gravestone for another individual.

By far the most unusual inscription found on a nineteenth century Ontario gravestone can be seen at Rushes Cemetery outside Crosshill (see photo on p. 67). Nearly the entire face of this marker is carved with a cryptogram. Aside from the family name, Bean, two women's names, Henrietta and Susanna, and "Gone Home," the only readable line on the marker is the sentence at the bottom, "Readers meet us in heaven." The marker is of the usual soft white marble and, as a result, many of the letters are now extremely difficult to decipher.

```
S  V  W  E  T  B  S . A  15 S  T  M  O   R  E .
E  I  R  T  E  2  Y  D  & H  N  S  10 H  E
M  A  A  D  17 & S  H  T  N  O  A  R  M  T
N  A  Y  D  H  D . N  E  F  S . M  Y  E  H  E
E  N  S . O  W  M . A  B  E  O  2  D  26 T  T
E  V  & E  I  R  O  M  I  F  S  G  E  E  E
H  R  S  27 D  I  I  E  T . W  R  7 . A  O  M
D . A  U  H  T  A  N  M  1  S  A  8  6  B . T
H  T  S  E  S  M  E  R  E  T  E  L  1  E  S .
Y  E  A  1  P . H  N  I  T  A  Y  R  I  P  M
E  W  N  8  6  5  A  G  E  D  23 A  P  E  L
E  R  N  H  S  N  W  F  W  O  I  D  T  D  H
I  G  A  I  2  D . I  E  H  D  E  27 H  G  O
T  F  R  M  O  A  D  R  N  W  N  E  V  N . A
F  S  O  G  D  N  A  E  O  I  H  A  E  M  Y
```

The solution to this cryptogram may be found in the Appendix at the end of the section of photographs.

Epitaphs, whether an appropriate standardized sentiment or a highly individualized creation, lend character to early Ontario gravestones. The epitaphs often read as if the deceased himself were speaking, though it is probable that he had little say in choosing his own epitaph. It is the rare person, now or then, who thinks in such specific terms about his own death as to choose his own grave-stone or epitaph. While an epitaph most likely did not directly reflect the deceased's ideas, it did reflect his personality as it was seen by the person who chose the memorial and decided its form. These distinctive memorials contrast sharply with modern machine-produced markers, regimented by mechanized techniques that leave little room for individuality.

The present-day monument maker receives his granite slabs pre-cut in a limited variety of simple geometric shapes and polished to a high gloss on at least one of the faces. The customer then chooses the style and size of lettering to be used and, providing the recipient cemetery has no regulations against it, he also chooses a design. Lettering styles and sizes as well as the design will usually be chosen from the monument maker's standard supply. The design and letters are transferred to the stone by use of a stencil-and-sandblasting method. First a pattern is made of paper or some similar material and affixed to the stone, then the stone is put on rollers and rolled into a room for sandblasting. Fine-grained sand is shot out of a nozzle by means of a powerful air or water current, and whatever area of the granite is exposed by the stencil will be cut away in a thin layer, creating a dull surface. When the pattern is removed, the part of the stone that was covered retains the shiny original finish. There are numerous minor variations of the method just described, but this is how the average modern gravestone is created at the average cost. Deviation from the norm will, of course, mean added cost.

Motifs

It is on gravestones of the 1830s, concurrent with the arrival of the professional stone carver, that decorative motifs begin to be found in increasing numbers. Before that time, most of the markers were carved only with matter-of-fact information—name, date of death, age, and often the name of the closest family relation. Decorative motifs became increasingly popular during the following twenty years, and by the middle of the century decorated markers were more usual than plain ones.

Five clear categories of motifs can be distinguished among the gravestones, with a sixth, Miscellaneous, category covering the rest. These motifs are: Classical Revival, Flowers, Hands, Animals and Angels.

Certainly there are markers on which these motif categories overlap, but generally these are groupings which can be easily recognized.

Though most of the motifs in all categories can be interpreted as Christian symbols, it must be remembered that Christian symbolism covers an enormous range of objects, animate and inanimate, and that it is often esoteric. Thus it may be a relatively simple matter to interpret a motif in complex, learned terms in an attempt to find serious, significant intent in the design of early gravestones; but in doing so one runs the risk of being quite wrong in interpreting the intent of the person who chose the motif for the gravestone. The average person was not a theologian, and motifs were chosen on the basis of suitability and personal inclination. Suitability entailed the aesthetic taste of the time. It reflected the tacit approval of church and community. It embraced that sense of decorum that plays so important a part in religious matters. Suitability was the conservative factor. Personal inclination and individualistic thoughts regarding the dead, were more or less dominated by what was suitable—more if the individual was interested in doing the acceptable and proper thing, less if he or she was headstrong. Suitability tended to win. Funerary art has always been a conservative one.

Turning to the motif categories, the first one, Classical Revival, is also the earliest one and reflects the same trend as that seen on United States gravestones of the same time period. During the first quarter of the nineteenth century, close on the heels of the neoclassical movement in Europe, North Americans became enamoured of the art and architecture of classical Greece. The trend was one of decorative embellishment rather than one of serious reinterpretation of form, and it brought to funerary art four common classical motifs—the willow, urn, column and obelisk. Though all these motifs appeared early and remained popular throughout the nineteenth century, it is the willow that remained the most popular motif on Ontario gravestones until the slab marker was abandoned just after the turn of the century.

As a Christian symbol, the willow represents the gospel of Christ because it is an exceptionally hardy tree, able to withstand the loss of many branches and still flourish— so, too, the gospel of Christ flourishes no matter how widely distributed among the peoples of the world. This esoteric symbolism undoubtedly escaped most who chose the willow as a grave marker's motif. To them the willow wept and, simultaneously, represented the tree of (eternal) life. As such it could be, and was, used in combination with a great variety of other motifs. Urns and obelisks most frequently appear with the willow, and either may be draped in mourning.

The second category, Flowers, was also widespread and took many forms in its representation of numerous species of flowers. It is true that many types of flowers are Christian symbols but, with the exception of the rose and the lily, their use on gravestones was most likely a natural extension of the traditional use of flowers to commemorate the dead. The rose and the lily are commonly recognized as being symbols of purity and were probably used in this sense as well as the commemorative one. Numerous examples of both flowers can be found on nineteenth century gravestones.

Judging from the great number of hand motifs that can be seen on the markers, this third category was second in popularity only to the willow and its classical acoutre-ments. Generally, hands took one of two forms—the hand pointing upward suggesting the path to heaven taken by the deceased, and two hands clasped, suggesting "God speed." The hand of God is an ancient and well-known symbol in the Christian religion and can be depicted in a variety of ways, leading the way to heaven or reaching down to earth. The motif of the hand descending from above is not common on Ontario gravestones though it can be seen on an occasional marker. The hand pointing heavenward is very popular, however, being a common motif from one end of the province to the other. The hand pointing heavenward can also be found on New England gravestones of the same period and may have been derived from that source. The clasping of hands has the symbolic meaning of union, though this motif on gravestones is often inscribed with the word "farewell." Thus it also symbolized human parting.

The fourth category, Animals, consists almost exclusively of lambs and doves. These figures were considered particularly suited to adorn children's gravestones and it is on their markers that the lamb or dove is most often found. Both are well known Christian symbols. As a symbol of Christ, the lamb has been one of the favorite and most frequently used symbols in all periods of Christian art. It also has various other interpretations within the Christian context. But because of its disproportionately frequent use on children's markers one might guess that a less traditional meaning had evolved, that youth and innocence were now being symbolized. The dove, in both pagan and Christian art, was the symbol of purity and peace.

The fifth category, Angels, scarcely needs explaining. Interestingly enough, angels were not as popular a motif as the willow or the hand. The angel motifs that do exist are most often found on children's graves.

Toward the end of the century motifs tended more and more toward the conventional contemporary funeral and Christian symbols—flowers, the open Bible and the cross. This narrow range of symbols became stereotyped and has survived to the present day as the most popular group of funerary motifs.

The Stones Today

Most nineteenth century markers are found in their original locations, though some communities have moved their old churchyard gravestones to present-day town cemeteries because of the requirements of upkeep or building expansion. Such is the case in both Kingston and St. Catharines, where large town cemeteries have special areas designated for the old markers to stand within the vast array of twentieth century stones.

The individuality of these markers, a factor that makes them so appealing to the modern beholder, was soundly based on a less hurried life. In the nineteenth century and before, cemeteries were meant to be visited. Grave markers were meant to be read, to evoke thought or simply to be enjoyed. So people took pleasant strolls through burying grounds and sat among the gravestones. Today a few cemeteries with old stones are being made into memorials for just this kind of use. The Upper Canada Village Pioneer Memorial is one of the best examples of the type. The old markers have been mounted into brick walls, and walkways circumscribe the whole. Other smaller memorials have been equally well done. The St. Andrew's Presbyterian churchyard in Streetsville is a charming example of a cemetery site that has been restored to create a protected setting for the old stones and a pleasant aspect for the visitor. The United Empire Loyalist Memorial in Adolphustown is equally well designed.

Most early Ontario gravestones will not last many more years if left untended. This survey has been an attempt to record some of them as they now stand.

The Plates

One of the few wooden grave markers still in existence is located in the White Chapel churchyard near Picton. Although there is no evidence of carved or painted lettering on the surface to determine its age, the churchyard in which it is situated contains only nineteenth century markers dating between 1827 and 1886. It is likely that this marker also dates from that period. The burial ground is no longer in use and, except for browsing deer whose hoof marks are visible in the photograph, it is seldom visited.

"Here lies the Remains of ALEXANDER GRANT Who Unfortunately
Perished upon Lake St. Francois the 22 Oct. 1794, Aged 37 Years."

Located in the St. Andrew's Church cemetery in Williamstown,
this is one of the earliest markers extant in Ontario. It is solid in
appearance, having somewhat bulky proportions and, considering
its age, is in an excellent state of preservation.

The simple wooden cross, that folkloric staple of pioneer burial
grounds, is not much in evidence in Ontario cemeteries, pioneer or
otherwise. This example stands in the main town cemetery of Niagara
Falls. An attempt at discovering the date of this marker was
unsuccessful, as the local historical society could locate no record of
an "Alexader Palamarnk."

The hand-carved quality of uneven lettering and spacing is very much in evidence on Hannah Nelles's gravestone, located with numerous like markers in the yard of St. Andrew's Anglican Church in Grimsby. A shortage of space led to the abbreviation of the word "please" to "pl" in the epitaph verse. Also, there appears to be an error in subtraction on the marker. According to the dates of birth and death, Hannah Nelles was thirty-two years old, not thirty, when she died.

In contrast to the preceding stone, the marker for "Jesse Page, Jun.," displays professional competence and craftsmanship in its carefully spaced and evenly cut lettering. Only eighteen years separate the two stones, giving evidence of the rapid rise of the monument maker's profession. This one is in the roadside cemetery between Union and Sparta.

"In Memory of Mary, wife, of Ashman Carpenter. She departed this Life, in the 80th Year of Her Age."

The remainder of the epitaph remains hidden in the tree trunk that at one time had enveloped Mary Carpenter's gravestone. The tree was recently cut down, revealing the stone. It is located in St. Andrew's Anglican churchyard in Grimsby.

Also in St. Andrew's Anglican churchyard in Grimsby is this
unusual arrangement of gravemarkers laid horizontally on uprights.
Other examples of this type of structure can be found scattered in
cemeteries across Ontario, but never in such quantity.

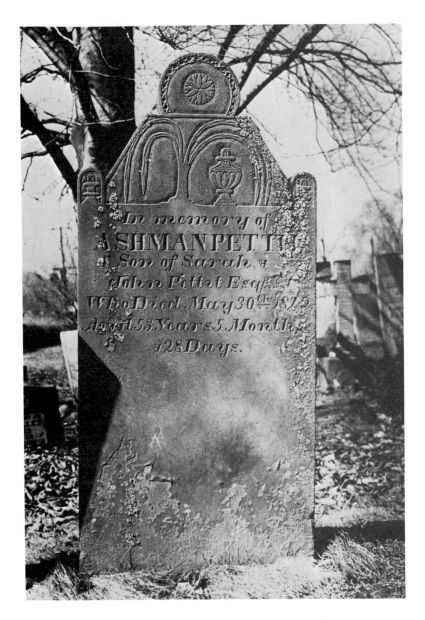

Willows, the single most popular gravestone motif in the nineteenth
century, took a variety of forms. The example on Ashman Pettit's
stone is more palm-like than most. This particular stylization is
retained on all the Pettit family stones standing in a row in the
St. Andrew's Anglican churchyard in Grimsby. All of these markers
are slate and therefore have kept a sharpness of image not
found on the white marble markers.

The Oriental appearance of the willow on this marker is unusual and perhaps a reflection of the interest in Chinese forms current in the United States a few years prior to this time. The stone lies flat on the ground, a fairly common way of installing slab markers, which are heavy in proportion to their narrow width. They are vunerable to breakage when placed upright. The problem in placing stones in this manner is obvious in the photograph. Vegetation overruns the edges of the marker and must be continually cut back if the stone is to remain uncovered. The marker is in St. Andrew's Church cemetery, Williamstown.

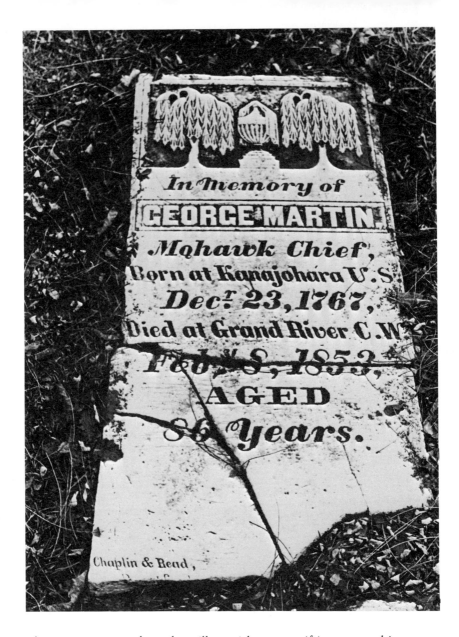

In Memory of
GEORGE MARTIN
Mohawk Chief,
Born at Kanajohára U:S:
Dec.ʳ 23, 1767,
Died at Grand River C.W
Feb.ʸ 8, 1853,
AGED
86 Years.

Chaplin & Bead,

A common approach to the willow-with-urn motif is seen on this marker in memory of George Martin, a Mohawk chief. The branches of the tree are shown with an abstract rendering of leaves. The urn sits on a pedestal between the two identical trees and is draped in mourning. The marker lies flat on the ground, perhaps placed in that position after it had been broken. It is located in the Mohawk Chapel burying ground in Brantford.

The Mohawk Chapel in Brantford has numerous nineteenth century grave markers scattered throughout the churchyard. As this burying ground is still in use, here one can see nineteenth and twentieth century markers side by side.

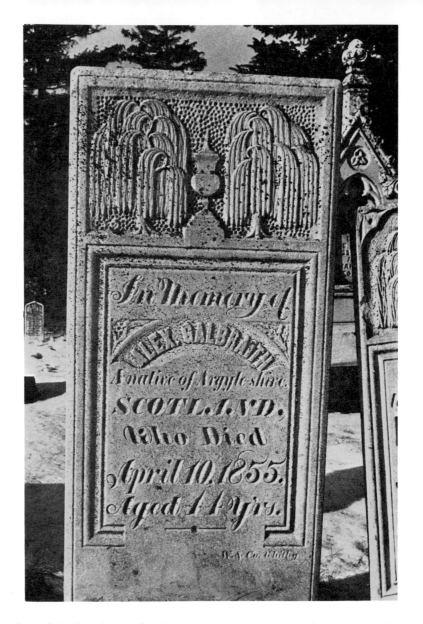

One of the hundreds of stylistic variations on the willow theme, this stone is similar in design to the preceding marker in memory of George Martin. Here the trees are abstracted in a different manner and the urn is not draped in mourning, but the composition within the pictorial design and of the entire marker remains similar.
The marker is found in the Bowmanville cemetery.

The willow accompanied by an obelisk is yet another variation on the Classical Revival theme to be found on early Ontario gravestones. This marker is located in the Presbyterian churchyard at Niagara-on-the-Lake.

A beautifully rendered, distinctively different treatment of the willow motif is seen on Archibald Davidson's marker located in the Brockville town cemetery. The ornate quality, the attention to detail, and the totality of the design that incorporates both motif and lettering make this marker an outstanding example of the beauty that can be found in nineteenth century gravestones.

Beautiful in its simplicity, this memorial to two-year-old Henry
Cornell is austere in design and small in size. It is one in the
collection of gravestones at Pioneer Village, a small grouping of early
Ontario buildings, situated between Kitchener and Doon.

The willow, simply used, is found with great frequency on gravestones throughout the province. Here it is found on a marker for a woman of German descent in the Hespeler town cemetery.

Occasionally the willow motif is incorporated into a larger pictorial narrative. On this marker for Margaret Conn, the willow becomes the background motif for the man, presumably Margaret's husband, seated in front of a representation of his wife's gravestone. The marker commemorates "also their infant." Death in childbirth was not uncommon in the nineteenth century and in this instance the infant also died.

The epitaph is illegible. The stone is in the Anglican cemetery belonging to St. Peter's Church, Tyrconnell.

"In loving remembrance of EDWARD JOSEPH DUKESBERY.
died Aug. 21, 1872. AE. 10 mo's. 24 days."

A frail and lovely flower was given
   Awhile to claim our care;
But now a cherub waits in heaven

   (The last line is below the ground)

Rarely are animals found in combination with any tree motif and
this is the only instance discovered of an animal depicted with a
willow. The identification of the animal is problematical as it has a
bovine appearance. While there is no precedent for a cow's being
depicted on a gravestone, given the already unusual circumstance
of an animal and a tree in juxtaposition on a single stone, the animal
here may indeed be a cow or possibly a lamb rendered in a style
peculiar to the stone carver. The epitaph offers no clue as it is a
standard epitaph verse for a child. The stone is located in the
Brockville cemetery.

An unusual combination of motifs can be seen on this marker in the cemetery located between Union and Sparta. A willow is the central motif, closely flanked by an urn on a pedestal and what may be an altar or a marker laid horizontally on uprights. The motifs on the outer edges are acorns with faces added for decoration. The whole is enclosed by a series of Gothic arches.

Willows in combination with the classic Greek urn are commonly found on nineteenth century markers. On this stone in the St. Andrew's Anglican churchyard in Grimsby, the addition of a wreath of laurel bordering the inscription is yet another aspect of the Classical Revival style. The epitaph is a passage from I Corinthians.

The classic Greek urn often stood alone or was used as a central motif. Here the decorative aspects of the Classical Revival style are extreme, the urn being flanked by foliage and fan-shaped accoutrements. The whole is topped by a shell design, much in the manner in which Greek temples were decorated at the apex of their roofline. The stone is in the Presbyterian churchyard, Niagara-on-the-Lake.

The epitaph is one that is not uncommon:

> Mourn not my wife and Children dear,
> I am not dead, but sleeping here;
> My loss are great, long is my rest,
> God called me home, He thought it best.

In Memory of

MARY BROOKFIELD

wife of

JACOB ZAVITZ

With the advent of the Classical Revival style in both art and architecture, the classic Greek urn became a popular gravestone motif. Traditionally a symbol of sorrow, it is shown either draped in mourning or not. The example pictured here is also flanked by an acorn and oak leaf on either side, the oak being an ancient symbol of the strength of faith and virtue. The stone is located in the roadside cemetery between Union and Sparta.

"ELIZA CATHARINE, Daughter of Robert & Mary WADDEL.
Died Sept. 5, 1838 AE. 17 yrs. 7 mo's. 12 ds.

"MARGARET ANN, Daughter of Robert & Mary WADDEL. Died
Dec 14, 1857, AE. . . . . 11 mo. 2 ds."

Floral motifs, often found in combination with other motifs, are
common. The wreath is particularly suited to combine with other
motifs because of its enclosing form and is here seen with an anchor,
symbol of hope. The marker stands in the Smithville cemetery.

61

Roses and lilies, symbols of purity, are used on this marker in combination with the hand pointing heavenward, a popular motif on nineteenth century Ontario gravestones. It is located in the Newcastle cemetery.

The epitaph reads:

> Young people all as you pass by,
> Think of me for you must die.
> Repent in time no time delay,
> I in my prime was called away.

The thistle, national flower of Scotland, was often used as a motif on stones marking the graves of Scottish immigrants. This example is located in the Presbyterian churchyard at Niagara-on-the-Lake.

In Memory of
Wᵐ CAMPBELL,
Died Apr. 2. 1854.
Æ. 89 yrs. & 1 mo.
Upon his left lies his wife
ELIZABETH BAKER
Died Dec. 27. 1842.
Æ. 72 yrs. & 3 mos.
Upon her left lies their Daughter
CATHARINE
Died Dec. 26. 1846.
Æ. 36 yrs. & 6 mos.

Originally from the Woodlands East cemetery, this marker was moved when waters from the St. Lawrence Seaway covered the cemetery. It is now mounted in the Pioneer Memorial at Upper Canada Village. Although flowers in a vase are not the most popular handling of the floral motif, when such a form is used it appears to be carefully and elaborately styled.

A few flowers in a vase decorate the Mallorytown gravestone of
Harriet Adell. One of the roses has fallen from the bouquet. This
stone was patched in a manner commonly seen today in the case of
old markers that are cared for. Iron clamps hold the two pieces
together and the break is filled with cement.

The hand pointing heavenward appears with great frequency on early
Ontario gravestones and at least once on a church steeple as well,
from the evidence pictured here. This church is in the Pioneer Village
between Kitchener and Doon and has, as an added precaution,
a lightning rod mounted behind the hand.

One of the most unusual markers dating from the nineteenth century is this one located in Rushes Cemetery near Crosshill. The epitaph consists almost entirely of a cryptogram with the exception of the sentence at the base of the stone which reads, "Readers meet us in heaven." The family name, Bean, and two women's names, Henrietta and Susanna, head the cryptogram, and the legend "Gone Home" is inscribed above the motif of the hand pointing heavenward.

The solution to the cryptogram is on p. 94.

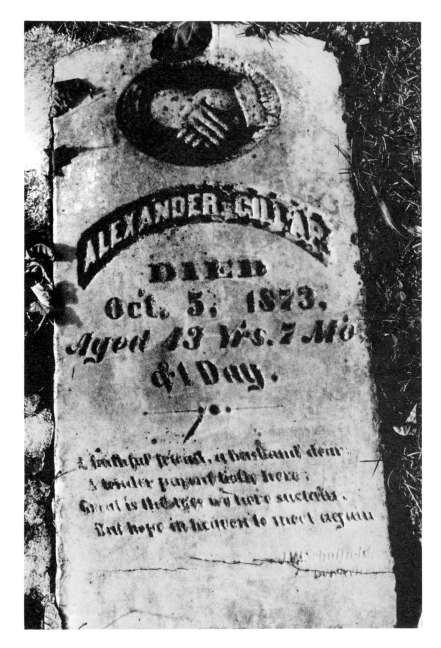

Another common form of the hand motif is that of clasped hands within an oval. The hands on this marker are typical of the form in both technique and style. The stone is in the Dunnville cemetery. The epitaph is also a common one.

> A faithful friend, a husband dear,
> A tender parent lieth here;
> Great is the loss we here sustain,
> But hope in heaven to meet again.

Not content with simply clasped hands, the designer of Stephen Bradley's gravestone added a death's-head and the ladder ascending to heaven. Both of these additional symbols were common in the New England states in the late eighteenth and early nineteenth centuries, but are most unusual in Canada. This marker is found in Niagara-on-the-Lake.

An example of the standard pointing-hand motif is found on the
Thomas Beattie marker located in St. Andrew's Presbyterian
churchyard in Streetsville. The addition of maple leaves flanking the
central motif is of interest here as it represents the only example
found of the maple leaf on any Ontario grave marker of this type.

The David Ross stone carries a seldom-used form of the hand motif.
The descending hand of God holds an open scroll that reads,
"Christ is the Resurrection and the Life." This marker is located
in the St. Andrew's Presbyterian churchyard in Streetsville.

This marker in the Bowmanville cemetery employs unusual variations on common motifs. The drapery of mourning has become a stage setting for the descending hand holding an open scroll. The torches of life on either side have been inverted.

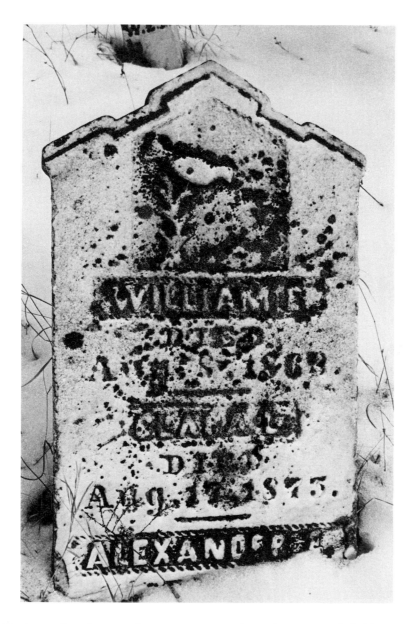

Birds are found most often on stones marking the graves of children. On this badly weathered stone that is also being covered by lichen growth, a small bird presides over the graves of three children, William E., Clara E. and Alexander E. The two legible dates are Aug. 8, 1863 and Aug. 17, 1875. The last date is hidden beneath the ground. The footstone for William is seen in the background, in the cemetery at Deseronto.

A motif found almost exclusively on children's gravestones is that of the lamb. The example pictured here is found in unusual combination with two hands pointing heavenward, for the two girls whose grave they mark. Also unusual is the use of the birth dates rather than the death dates of the girls. The marker is located in the roadside cemetery between Union and Sparta.

One of the most common forms of the lamb motif is this example,
located in the cemetery between Union and Sparta. As with
many of the markers in this cemetery, this one has sunk far enough
into the ground to eliminate the bottom few lines of the inscription.

Frequent examples of sculptured lambs are found marking the graves
of children. However, owing to the soft nature of the marble from
which they are carved, by the time they are a hundred years old
they have lost much of their original detail. This example is located
in the town cemetery at St. Catharines.

Much of this marker has sunk beneath the ground. All that is now visible of the inscription reads, "To the Memory of JOHN." The two motifs employed are most unusual and found only on one other marker, which is located in the same cemetery. The stag, in Christian context, represents piety, religious aspiration, solitude and purity of life—rather esoteric symbolism in light of what is usually found on nineteenth century Ontario gravestones. The tree, obviously not a willow, may be an oak, ancient symbol of the strength of faith and virtue, or an elm, Christian symbol of the dignity of life. In either case the combination of motifs is uncommon and seemingly erudite. The marker is in the Woodhouse United Church cemetery near Vittoria.

Two nearly identical markers for members of the McLean family are located in St. Andrew's Anglican churchyard in Grimsby.

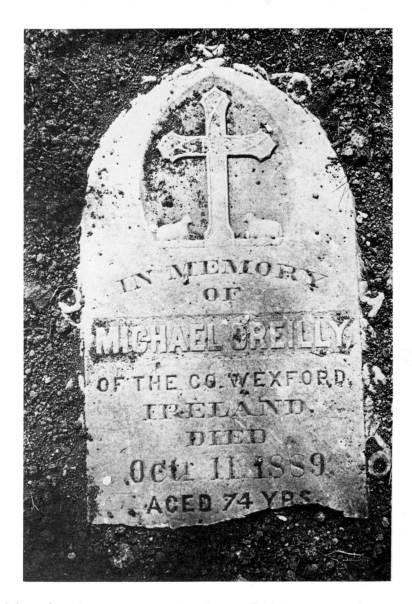

IN MEMORY
OF
MICHAEL OREILLY
OF THE CO. WEXFORD,
IRELAND,
DIED
Octr 11 1889.
AGED 74 YRS.

More often than not it seems that Roman Catholic grave markers are carved with crosses, either as part of a larger decorative scheme or as a single motif. This example of a cross flanked by two lambs is found in St. Mary's Cemetery in Kingston.

"In Memory of JOHN Son of James H & Maria Mandeville.
Who Died Feby 25, 1848: AE 15 Y: 1 M: 5 Dy:"

In addition to bird and lamb motifs, angels are often found on
children's gravestones. The charmingly expressive faces of these angels
and the fineness of detail, as yet untouched by the weathering
process, combine to make this marker an outstanding example of the
motif. What the weather has not destroyed, however, fungi eventually
will. The black fungus at the base of the stone loosens the surface
layers of the rock until both fungus and rock flake away. The grey
fungus at the top will eventually obliterate the design. This marker
is in St. John's Anglican churchyard near Simcoe.

In the Mallorytown cemetery there are a surprising number of obelisk grave markers, an example of how a particular form can find favor in an area. On this one, for a little girl, is added an angel. Fungus growth has all but obliterated the epitaph at the base of this marker.

It is apparent that most early Ontario gravestones fit readily into
categories based on the type of motif carved onto their face. There
are a few motifs, however, that are either unique or are seen in
unusual enough combinations to avoid categorization. The burning
altar, for example, though not an unknown symbol, is unusual among
early Ontario markers, perhaps because of its association with Jewish
ritual as an altar of burnt offerings. Considering the motifs separately,
fire is symbolic of martyrdom and religious fervor, the altar and altar
cloth represent the presence of Christ and Christ's shroud. This
stone has been repaired by means of two iron bands bolted on either
side, cutting off part of the name, Peter, and the date of death.
It is in St. Paul's Anglican Burying Ground, Caledonia.

Angel motifs take many forms. Seldom are two alike. The Maria Fus stone, located in the Hespeler cemetery, marks the grave of a mother and her son. Many stones in the Hespeler cemetery reflect the German origin of the early inhabitants of that region in the use of the German language for the inscriptions. The pictorial elements, however, show the same range of motifs and styles as do all other early Ontario gravestones.

"SACRED to the memory of KATHARINE LOUISA Daughter of
Joseph Ives and Katharine Echa . . . who departed this life on the
13th of November 1835. Aged . . . years 2 months 15 days. To the
inexpressible grief of her afflicted Parents."

The awkwardness of these shaggy-haired angels with their cape-like
wings only enhances the charm of this marker to Katharine Louisa
located in St. John's Anglican churchyard near Simcoe. Fortunately
the pictorial motif is relatively untouched by the fungi that are
closing in on the rest of the stone, making the text difficult to read.
A few letters and the age of the girl are already undecipherable. The
angels are more shallowly carved than usual and as a result will be
soon worn away by the action of the weather.

The mourning angel became a somewhat more common sculptural
form at the end of the nineteenth century and the beginning of
the twentieth century than it had been as a two-dimensional motif
before that time. This marker is located in the roadside cemetery
between Union and Sparta.

"In memory of MARY VANRIPER Consort of Albert Terhune
who died Dec. 15th, 1839 Aged 71 years and 10 days. Blessed are the
dead which die in the Lord. Blessed with every virtue which enobles.
Adorn the christian, friend and wife . . ." (The remainder of the
epitaph is below the ground.)

This marker, rich in unusual symbolism, stands in the Woodhouse
United churchyard outside Vittoria. The trumpeting angel is almost
never to be found on gravestones in Canada or the United States
during the nineteenth century. The hourglass, however, with its
sands of time run out, is a common motif on New England gravestones
of this period and earlier. The grapevine is a vivid Biblical symbol
used either as an emblem of Christ or to express the relationship
between God and mankind.

Picturing the deceased in his coffin was far more common in New England markers of the eighteenth century than it was on Ontario markers of the nineteenth century. The occurance of the motif on this marker in St. Mary's Cemetery in Kingston would appear to be unique in Ontario.

"To the memory of the Revd Patk Neelan who died of fever contracted in the discharge of his ministry to the sick on the 26th day of July 1847. Aged 26 years."

The Irish, fleeing the potato famine of 1847, crammed into ships sailing to North America and fell victims to a typhus epidemic as a result of the terrible conditions aboard ship. An estimated 16,000 people died that summer, 1,400 of them in Kingston.

This marker to Jemima Howick combines a number of motifs in a beautifully designed manner. A dove descends from heaven with an olive branch. An hourglass, trumpet and book, most likely the Bible, complete the composition. The marker is at Woodhouse United Church outside Vittoria.

The epitaph reads:

> We must all appear before the judgement
> soul of Christ that every one may
> receive the things done in the body acco-
> rding to that he hath done.

The open book, often with a brief Biblical inscription, begins to appear toward the end of the nineteenth century. This example from the Smithville cemetery, dated 1862, is an early form of what became a popular motif in the twentieth century. The marker is almost hidden in the summer when the hedge that grows around it is in leaf. Both inscription and epitaph are nearly illegible.

A heap of broken, discarded markers in the corner of the Brantford cemetery is visible proof of the destruction of early Ontario gravestones through neglect.

Neglect of markers can also have a benign effect. These stones stand
beneath St. Paul's Church parish hall in Kingston. Built in 1872,
the hall was constructed over part of the church burying ground.
A few markers were apparently broken in the process, and a total
of twelve were roofed over by the building. Three of them remain
standing in the unfinished basement today. The nine that were
knocked over and broken lie among the dirt and debris of the
basement. But, since all have been protected from the weather since
1872, their surfaces are in clearly legible condition.

Photos by Haak Bakken

Preservation of old gravestones by this method is not uncommon.
The markers are moved from their original location and placed close
together in rows on a cement slab. This group is located along
Highway 6 that crosses the Bruce Peninsula.

Appendix: The Solution to the Cryptogram

The cryptogram found in Rushes Cemetery at Crosshill can be read by following the direction of the lines on the chart below. The cryptogram measures fifteen letters across and fifteen letters down. The inscription begins approximately in the center, at the seventh letter across and the seventh letter down which is circled in the diagram.

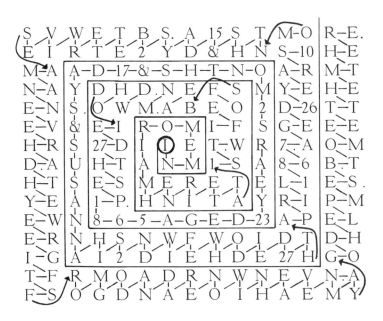

It reads, "In Memoriam. Henrietta, 1st wife of S. Bean, M.D., who died 27th Sep. 1865, aged 23 years, 2 months & 17 days & Susanna, his 2nd wife, who died 27th April 1867, aged 26 years 10 months & 15 days. 2 better wives a man never had. They were gifts from God and are now in Heaven. May God help me, S.B., to meet them there."